MW00474061

BEING

*Other inspirational books
by Susan Hayward*

A Guide For The Advanced Soul
Begin It Now
Bag of Jewels

Published by In-Tune Books

BEING

Created and Edited
by

SUSAN HAYWARD

HAYWARD BOOKS
An Imprint of In-Tune Books,
Sydney. Australia

HAYWARD BOOKS
An Imprint of In-Tune Books
PO Box 193 Avalon Beach,
NSW 2107 Australia.
www.haywardbooks.com
email: questions@haywardbooks.com

First Published in Australia November 1997
US & UK EDITION November 2002

B E I N G
Copyright © 1997 by Susan Hayward
All rights reserved.
Compilation copyright of Author.

Jacket Design & Concept by Susan Hayward
Typography by Seymours Design
Title Calligraphy by Margaret Laysom
Produced by Phoenix Offset, HK.

ISBN 0 9590439 8 5

By the same author:
A GUIDE FOR THE ADVANCED SOUL   0 9577025 15
BEGIN IT NOW   0959 0439 4 2
BAG OF JEWELS   0959 0439 6 9

International Distributors:

AUST	HarperCollins Publishers
UK	Bertrams, Gardiners, WLM
NZ	HarperCollins Publishers
USA	Words Distributing, Bookpeople,
	New Leaf Ingrams Distribution

DEDICATED

TO

Malcolm, Zaky and Autumn
~My angels here on Earth~

and to you,
To the infinite possibilities of your Being
and the truth, beauty and wisdom of
your own soul

~

Foreword

"What is this world without a further Divine purpose in it all!"

Walt Whitman

This book is a collection of timeless works of art and literature, left to humanity by men and woman who had great Being. Why do their creations endure throughout the centuries? I believe they created their works in higher states of consciousness. Their work is imperishable because it was created in the moment, in a state of full self awareness. If you are in the present moment when viewing a Leonardo da Vinci painting, you see eternity, because it was created in a moment of eternity. Because of their high level of consciousness, the Gods used these 'conscious beings' for divine teachings to assist man's evolution here on earth.

What is Being? Being is the expression of who you are. It is your level of consciousness, and how much you know and understand your real self. Have you ever recognised something special in a person, something that suggested they had great depth of soul? It is hard to define, but you *feel* it. Through their life experiences, they have created will and understanding, raising their level of Being.

Life is a test of your Being, and Being is accumulated though experiences of adversity. Our soul grows through trials and sorrow. Everybody suffers in some way with pain, sadness, grief, depression and loneliness. We need friction to produce consciousness, and suffering is the payment for the process of evolution.

All great philosophies say suffering is a part of the human condition, that it gives us strength. The message within this book however suggests that one must not suffer *unnecessarily*. Rather, one can strive to transform it into higher consciousness. How? *By acceptance of what the Gods give us.*. Only through the acceptance of suffering can you rise above it. Suffering is increased by your resistance to it, by trying to run from it. The only way is to embrace it. We can *use* our suffering to create Being.

The personal growth movement of our times is about avoiding suffering and making your life full of only positive experiences. It suggests that we can have the perfect job, the perfect relationship, unlimited wealth, getting all you want right now. But it is the obstacles and difficulties in life that create Being, and we are here because we *are* imperfect. Instead of focussing on trying to get what we want, we can try to know who we really are.

I endured a great deal of friction in the process of creating this book. It was if I needed to experience much suffering to raise my level of Being, to earn the right to publish this book from the truth of who I am. At one moment I thought my daughter was going to die - it was a shock given by the Gods as an opportunity to separate from the fear and try to be in the present. Many times in the past few months I have had to remind myself to accept events, to understand that they do not last forever, and to allow them to run their course.

The conscious beings within this book all had great suffering in their lives. But by separating from their suffering - not 'being' the suffering - they allowed themselves to express the Divine. They truly understood that they had a role to play in their lifetime, and they accepted this role with humility. A common theme in this book is that we all have our destinies, that we do not live life, *but life lives us.* Perhaps our lives are simply roles we play to evolve, and are not to be taken seriously. We have our unchosen fate, and all we can change is our consciousness.

What we read in 'Being', in some instances, is written in esoteric language: the words are not literal, but have hidden spiritual meanings. The works of art too have psychological meaning, the artists having used symbolism to express eternal truths. The teachings left behind by these highly evolved beings are secret instructions for life and the inner development of man. They wrote in metaphors and parables to withstand the interpretations of many translators, so that the esoteric truths would not be lost forever. Reading some poetry, you may not understand with your mind, but your inner intuitive self recognises something higher. The words reach your soul on a deep level.

This book is only a sample of my favourite literature and paintings. They are reminders from the Gods to help me live more consciously. Because of the nature of this book, it was necessary to take fragments and extracts from the chosen selections. I hope this sample will encourage you to seek out the wonderful volumes that have been saved for posterity. To behold the original paintings shown in this book some-time in your life is a wonderful aim. Viewing them makes you feel your own divine essence, and the intangibility of life here.

One of my aims for this book was to create a compilation of quality literature and images to lift your spirit and nourish your Being. We waste so much of our precious spare time, so my intention was to produce a book of fine impressions that could be carried with you anywhere as a travelling compan-ion. So much beauty and artistic wealth is available to us, yet we fill our lives with lower impressions that do not give us a sense of the beauty of ourselves and the world.

So may these immortal words and images permeate <u>your</u> Being and reach the truth of who you are. May they touch your inner light so that it will shine forth from you with increasing Being.

With every blessing,

Susan Hayward

Whatever may happen to you,
it was prepared for you from all eternity
and the implication of causes was
from eternity spinning the
thread of your being,
and of that which is incident to it.

MARCUS AURELIUS

Cartoon for St. Anne, the Virgin, the Infant Christ and the Young St. John
LEONARDO DA VINCI, The National Gallery, London

From time to time one reaches the point
where the pressure of life
    seems almost unbearable.

The important thing is to keep the flavour
of the new and the longing for the
miraculous
    in spite of everything.

RODNEY COLLIN
The Theory of Conscious Harmony

We are not to lead a life that is not tested.

EPICTETUS

The present will have its rights.
   If one seizes the present, and treats with a freshness
   of feeling what is offered one, one almost
   always makes sure of something good,
   and if one sometimes does not succeed,
   one has, at least, lost nothing.

Hold fast by the present.
   Every situation-nay, every moment- is of infinite worth,
   for it is the representative of a whole eternity.

J.W. VON GOETHE

Providence has a myriad means to raise
the fallen and support the prostrate.

Sometimes our fate resembles a fruit tree in winter.
Who would think at beholding so sad a sight
that these rigid branches, these jagged twigs,
would turn green again in the spring
and blossom and bear fruit?

But we hope it, we know it!

J.W. VON GOETHE

It is a permanent principle
that one has to work
beyond one's capacities to
change one's level of being.

P.D. OUSPENSKY

I want to beseech you…to be patient
  toward all that is unsolved in your heart
    and to try to love *the questions themselves*
      like locked rooms and like books
        that are written in a very foreign tongue.

Do not now seek the answers,
  which cannot be given you
    because you would not be able to live them.
      And the point is, to live everything.
        Live the questions now.

      Perhaps you will then gradually,
        without noticing it,
          evolve some distant day
            into the answer.

RAINER MARIA RILKE
Letters to a Young Poet
Translated by M. D. Herter Norton

I think prayer, or some appeal from the whole
    heart to a force outside our circle of life
    which alone can alter things there,
    is the only possibility in certain
    insoluble circumstances.

But surely we must cry to be shown the way out,
    to be shown the unseen ladder out of the impasse,
    and be very ready to accept whatever is shown.

Then if some new idea, some new light
    comes into one's heart - as it will -
    one must be prepared to obey courageously.

If one does so,
    one will be led out of the maze.

RODNEY COLLIN
The Theory of Conscious Harmony

The Virgin of the Rocks (detail)
LEONARDO DA VINCI, The National Gallery, London

$\mathbf{I}$t is not for show that our soul
must enact its part;

it is at home, within us,
where no eyes penetrate
but our own.

MICHEL MONTAIGNE

Head of a Woman
LEONARDO DA VINCI, The Royal Collection,
© Her Majesty The Queen, Windsor Castle

The First Elegy
(excerpt)

Of course, it is strange to inhabit the
 earth no longer,
to give up customs one barely had
 time to learn,
not to see roses and other promising
 Things
in terms of a human future; no longer
 to be
what one was in infinitely anxious
 hands; to leave
even one's own first name behind,
 forgetting it
as easily as a child abandons a broken
 toy.

Strange to no longer desire one's
    desires. Strange
to see meanings that clung together
    once, floating away
in every direction. And being dead is
    hard work
and full of retrieval before one can
    gradually feel
a trace of eternity.- Though the living
    are wrong to believe
in the too-sharp distinctions which
    they themselves have created.
Angels (they say) don't know whether
    it is the living
they are moving among, or the dead.
    The eternal torrent
whirls all ages along in it, through
    both realms
forever, and their voices are drowned
    out in its thunderous roar.

RAINER MARIA RILKE
The First Elegy (excerpt)
Translated by Stephen Mitchell

If thou shalt strive to live only
what is truly thy life, that is,
the present,
then thou wilt be able to pass that portion of life
which remains for thee up to the time of thy death,
free from perturbations,
nobly, and obedient
to the god that is within thee.

MARCUS AURELIUS

All circumstances, good or bad, must change in time.

If one can only pass through them equally,
   without being borne too much up or too much down,
   one becomes ready for other changes.

      It is not the happy or tragic role that makes the
      difference between actors,
         but the way the role is played.

RODNEY COLLIN
The Theory of Conscious Harmony

Every glorious creation, every great discovery,
every thought that bears fruit and leads to results,
they are all beyond any man's control
and above all earthly power.

We must take them as unhoped-for heavenly gifts,
unspoilt children of God whom
we ought to welcome and honour,
gladly and thankfully.

They are akin to the Daimonic,
that overwhelming Power which
does with man as it chooses,
and to which he surrenders unconsciously,
believing that he is acting on his own impulse.

In such cases a man must be considered as
   the tool of a higher world-order,
   a vessel found worthy to receive
   divine influences.

I say this remembering how often
   a single idea has changed the character
   of centuries,
   and how individuals, through what flowed
   from them, have left a mark on their age
   lasting through generations and working
   on for good.

J.W. VON GOETHE

The thought of God — most neglected in life of all
humanity's attributes, easily cover'd with dust,
deluded and abused, rejected,
	yet the only certain source of what all are seeking,
	but few or none find.

	I say whoever labors here,
makes contributions here,
or best of all sets an incarnated example here,
	in life or death,
is dearest to humanity —
remains after the rest are gone.

WALT WHITMAN

However much we are attracted and fascinated
by the myriad phenomena of this earth,
an inner longing compels us
again and again
to turn our eye heavenward

because an inexplicable deep feeling convinces us
that we are citizens of those worlds
that mysteriously shine above us
and that we shall some day return thither.

J.W. VON GOETHE

What is the price of experience?
Do men buy it for a song?
Or wisdom for a dance in the street?

No,
it is bought with the price of all that a man hath,
his house, his wife, his children.

Wisdom is sold in the desolate market
where none come to buy,
and in the withered field
where the farmer ploughs for bread in vain.

WILLIAM BLAKE

Self-Portrait 1657 REMBRANDT HARMENSZ VAN RIJN,
Duke of Sutherland Collection/National Gallery of Scotland, Edinburgh

The most difficult thing -but an essential one -
is to love Life,
to love it even while one suffers,
because Life is all.

Life is God, and to love Life means
to love God.

LEO TOLSTOY

For in much wisdom is much grief:
and he that increaseth knowledge
increaseth sorrow.

ECCLESIASTES 1:18

Things cannot fall from heaven,
they cannot be found,
they must be bought.

What one can get is proportionate to
what one is prepared to pay.
And one has to pay in advance;
there is no credit.

P.D. OUSPENSKY

There's a special providence
    in the fall of a sparrow.
    If it be now, 't is not to come;
    if it be not to come, it will be now;
    if it be not now, yet it will come:
    the readiness is all.

Since no man has aught of what he leaves,
    what is't to leave betimes?
    Let be.

WILLIAM SHAKESPEARE
Hamlet

The Ninth Elegy
(excerpt)

But because *truly* being here is so much; because everything here
apparently needs us, this fleeting world, which in some strange way
keeps calling to us. Us, the most fleeting of all.
Once for each thing. Just once; no more. And we too,
just once. And never again. But to have been
this once, completely, even if only once:
to have been at one with the earth, seems beyond undoing.

And so we keep pressing on, trying to achieve it,
trying to hold it firmly in our simple hands,
in our overcrowded gaze, in our speechless heart.
Trying to overcome it. - Whom can we give it to? We would
hold on to it all, forever ..... Ah, but what can we take along
into that other realm? Not the art of looking,
which is learned so slowly, and nothing that happened here. Nothing.
The sufferings, then. And, above all, the heaviness,
and the long experience of love, —just what is wholly
unsayable. But later, among the stars,
what good is it - *they* are *better* as they are: unsayable.

For when the traveller returns from the mountain-slopes into the valley,
he brings, not a handful of earth, unsayable to others, but instead
some word he has gained, some pure word, the yellow and blue
gentian. Perhaps we are *here* in order to say: house,
bridge, fountain, gate, pitcher, fruit-tree, window—
at most: column, tower ....But to say them, you must understand,
oh to say them *more* intensely than the Things themselves
ever dreamed of existing. Isn't the secret intent
of this taciturn earth, when it forces lovers together,
that inside their boundless emotion all things may shudder with joy?
Threshold: what it means for two lovers
to be wearing down, imperceptibly, the ancient threshold of their door -
they too, after the many who came before them
and before those to come ......,lightly.

RAINER MARIA RILKE
The Ninth Elegy (excerpt)
Translated by Stephen Mitchell

Must we barely arrive at this beginning of us? -
and yet it is enough, O soul;
O soul, we have positively appear'd-
that is enough.

WALT WHITMAN
As the Time Draws Nigh

There is nothing so beautiful and legitimate
    as to play the part of a man properly;

there is no knowledge as hard to acquire
    as the knowledge of how
    to live this life naturally,

and the most barbarous of our maladies
    is to despise our being.

MICHEL MONTAIGNE

The greater the power that deigns to serve you,
the more honour it demands of you.

SOCRATES

The School of Athens (detail of Plato and Aristotle) RAPHAEL,
The Vatican Museums & Galleries, Rome

We cannot obtain heavenly bliss
through our strength alone,
but with the assistance of divine grace;
and man, despite all his follies and errors,
being led by a higher hand,
reaches some happy goal at last.

J.W. VON GOETHE

Each of us living beings is a puppet of the gods.
Whether we have been constructed to serve
as their plaything
or for some serious reason
is beyond our power to know.

PLATO

To be, or not to be: that is the question:
   Whether 't is nobler in the mind to suffer
   The slings and arrows of outrageous fortune,
   Or to take arms against a sea of troubles,
   And by opposing end them?

To die: to sleep; No more;
   and by a sleep to say we end
   The heart-ache and the thousand natural shocks
   That flesh is heir to,
   't is a consummation devoutly to be wish'd.

To die, to sleep;
   To sleep: perchance to dream: ay, there's the rub;
   For in that sleep of death what dreams may come
   When we have shuffled off this mortal coil,
   Must give us pause. There's the respect
   That makes calamity of so long life;

For who would bear the whips and scorns of time,
  the oppressor's wrong, the proud man's contumely,
  The pangs of disprized love, the law's delay,
  The insolence of office, and the spurns
  That patient merit of the unworthy takes,
  When he himself might his quietus make
  With a bare bodkin?

Who would fardels bear,
  To grunt and sweat under a weary life,
  But that the dread of something after death,
  The undiscovered country from whose bourn
  No traveller returns, puzzles the will,
  And makes us rather bear those ills we have
  Than fly to others that we know not of?
  Thus conscience does make cowards of us all;

And thus the native hue of resolution
  Is sicklied o'er with the pale cast of thought,
  And enterprises of great pith and moment
  With this regard their currents turn awry,
  And lose the name of action.

WILLIAM SHAKESPEARE
Hamlet

One must manage one's life in order to enjoy it.

I enjoy my life more than others,
    for the measure of enjoyment depends
    upon the greater or lesser attention that we lend it.

Especially at the moment when I perceive
    that my life is so brief, I try to increase its mass;
    I try to arrest the speed of its flight by
    the speed with which I grasp it, and to
    compensate for the haste of its ebb by my
    vigour in using it.

The shorter my possession of life,
    the deeper and fuller I must make it.

MICHEL MONTAIGNE

It is my business
to manage carefully and dexterously
whatever happens.

EPICTETUS

I am under the direction of Messengers
    from Heaven, Daily and Nightly,
      but the nature of such things is not,
        as some suppose, without trouble or care.

Temptations are on the right hand and left;
behind, the sea of time and space roars and
follows swiftly;
he who keeps not right onwards is lost,
and if our footsteps slide in clay,
how can we do otherwise than fear and tremble!

But if we fear to do
    the dictates of our Angels,
      and tremble at the tasks set before us,
      if we refuse to do Spiritual Acts
because of Natural Fears and Desires!
Who can describe the dismal torment
of such a state!

WILLIAM BLAKE

The Annunciation (detail)
LEONARDO DA VINCI, Galleria Degli Uffizi, Florence

No one escapes destiny.

PLATO

The Annunciation (detail)
LEONARDO DA VINCI, Galleria Degli Uffizi, Florence

You are a primary existence.
You are a distinct portion of the essence of God
and contain a certain part of Him in yourself.

Why then are you ignorant of your noble birth?
You carry a God about within you, poor wretch,
and know nothing of it.

EPICTETUS

From
The Sonnets to Orpheus

A god can do it. But will you tell me how
a man can enter through the lyre's strings?
Our mind is split. And at the shadowed crossing
of heart-roads, there is no temple for Apollo.

Song, as you have taught it, is not desire,
not wooing any grace that can be achieved;
song is reality. Simple, for a god.
But when can *we* be real? When does he pour

the earth, the stars, into us? Young man,
it is not your loving, even if your mouth
was forced wide open by your own voice—learn

to forget that passionate music. It will end.
True singing is a different breath, about
nothing. A gust inside the god. A wind.

RAINER MARIA RILKE
Sonnet I,3
Translated by Stephen Mitchell

We talk far too much.
   The more I think of it, there is something
   futile about speech.

How the quiet gravity of nature
   and her silence
      by contrast startles one
         when one faces her collected.

J.W. VON GOETHE

$\mathcal{A}$ thought — the thought that wakes in silent hours —
   perhaps the deepest, most eternal thought
   latent in the human soul —
   this is the thought of God, merged in the
   thoughts of moral right
   and the immortality of identity.

   Great, great is this thought —
         – aye, greater than all else.

WALT WHITMAN

People have (with the help of conventions)
   oriented all their solutions toward the easy
   and toward the easiest side of the easy;
   but it is clear that we must *hold to what is difficult*;

everything alive holds to it, everything in Nature
   grows and defends itself in its own way and is
   characteristically and spontaneously itself,
   seeks at all costs to be so and against all opposition.

We know little,
   but that we must hold to what is difficult is a
   certainty that will not forsake us;
   it is good to be solitary, for solitude is difficult;

that some thing is difficult
   must be a reason the more for us to do it.

RAINER MARIA RILKE
*from Letters To A Young Poet
Translated by M.D. Herter Norton*

Much suffering in human life results
from a fruitless attempt to retain a note
that has already ceased to sound,
or to anticipate a note
that has not yet sounded.

RODNEY COLLIN
The Theory of Conscious Harmony

If a man should conquer in battle
a thousand and a thousand more,
and another should conquer himself,
his would be the greater victory,

because the greatest of victories
is the victory over oneself;
and neither the gods in heaven above
nor the demons down below can turn
into defeat the victory of such a man.

THE BUDDHA

Neither does anyone, however many
wounds he may have received, die,
unless he has run his allotted term of life:
nor does any man,
though he sits quietly by the fireside
under his own roof,
escape the more his fated doom.

AESCHYLUS

$\mathcal{M}$ay such calm of soul be mine,
so as to meet the force of circumstances.

AESCHYLUS

Titus in friar's habit 1660
REMBRANDT HARMENSZ VAN RIJN, Rijksmuseum, Amsterdam

When I consider every thing that grows
Holds in perfection but a little moment,
That this huge stage presenteth nought but shows
Whereon the stars in secret influence comment;
When I perceive that men as plants increase,
Cheered and check'd even by the self-same sky,
Vaunt in their youthful sap, at height decrease,
And wear their brave state out of memory;
Then the conceit of this inconstant stay
Sets you most rich in youth before my sight,
Where wasteful Time debateth with Decay,
To change your day of youth to sullied night;
And all in war with Time for love of you,
As he takes from you, I engraft you new.

WILLIAM SHAKESPEARE
Sonnet XV

I have observed that all intelligent people
recognise, some in a refined
and some in an unrefined way,

that the moment is everything.

J.W. VON GOETHE

Grand is the Seen

Grand is the seen, the light, to me - grand are the
    sky and stars,
Grand is the earth, and grand are lasting time and space,
And grand their laws, so multiform, puzzling, evolutionary;
But grander far the unseen soul of me, comprehending,
    endowing all those,
Lighting the light, the sky and stars, delving the earth, sailing
    the sea,
(What were all those, indeed, without thee, unseen soul? of
    what amount without thee?)
More evolutionary, vast, puzzling, O my soul!
More multiform far - more lasting thou than they.

WALT WHITMAN
Leaves of Grass

Our birth is but a sleep and a forgetting;
The Soul that rises with us, our life's Star,
Hath had elsewhere its setting
And cometh from afar;
Not in entire forgetfulness,
And not in utter nakedness,
But trailing clouds of glory do we come
From God, who is our home:
Heaven lies about us in our infancy!
Shades of the prison - house begin to close
Upon the growing boy,
But he beholds the light, and whence it flows,
He sees it in his joy;
The youth, who daily farther from the east
Must travel, still is Nature's priest,
And by the vision splendid
Is on his way attended;
At length the man perceives it die away,
And fade into the light of common day.

WILLIAM WORDSWORTH
Ode On Intimations Of Immortality

If we examine every stage of our lives we find that
from our first breath to our last we are
under the constraint of circumstances.

And yet we still possess the greatest of all freedoms, the
power of developing our innermost selves in harmony
with the moral order of the universe and so winning
peace at heart whatever obstacles we meet.

It is easy to say this and to write this.
But it always remains a task to
which every day must be devoted.

Every morning cries to us:
"Do what you ought and trust what may be."

J.W. VON GOETHE

With whatever pattern
you find yourself inwardly blended
(even a moment out of the life of pain),
feel that the whole,
the glorious carpet's intended.

RAINER MARIA RILKE
Excerpt from Sonnet 12
The Sonnets to Orpheus

Continue to make demands of the day your
   immediate concern and take occasion to test the
   purity of your heart and the steadfastness of your spirit.

When you then take a deep breath and rise above the cares
   of the world in an hour of leisure, you will
   surely win the right frame of mind to face devoutly
   what is above us, with reverence,
   seeing in all events the manifestations
   of a higher guidance.

J.W. VON GOETHE

Things are as they are
and will be brought to the issue destined.

AESCHYLUS

The First Elegy
(excerpt)

Who, if I cried out, would hear me among the angels'
hierarchies? and even if one of them
pressed me
suddenly against his heart: I would be
consumed
in that overwhelming existence. For
beauty is nothing
but the beginning of terror, which we
still are just able to endure,
and we are so awed because it serenely
disdains
to annihilate us. Every angel is
terrifying.

Angel beating a drum (detail from the Linaivoli Triptych)
FRA ANGELICO, Museo Di San Marco Dell' Angelico, Florence

And so I hold myself back and
  swallow the call-note
of my dark sobbing. Ah, whom can we
  ever turn to
in our need? Not angels, not humans,
and already the knowing animals are
  aware
that we are not really at home in
our interpreted world. Perhaps there
  remains for us
some tree on a hillside, which every
  day we can take
into our vision; there remains for us
  yesterday's street
and the loyalty of a habit so much
  at ease
when it stayed with us that it moved
  in and never left.

Oh and night: there is night, when
a wind full of infinite space
gnaws at our faces. Whom would it
not remain for - that longed-after,
mildly disillusioning presence, which
the solitary heart
so painfully meets. Is it any less
difficult for lovers?
But they keep on using each other
to hide their own fate.
    Don't you know yet? Fling the
emptiness out of your arms
into the spaces we breathe; perhaps
the birds
will feel the expanded air with more
passionate flying.

RAINER MARIA RILKE
The First Elegy (excerpt)
Translated by Stephen Mitchell

When you are troubled about anything,
   you have forgotten this,
   that all things happen
   according to universal nature;

and forgotten this,
   that a man's wrongful act is nothing to you;

and further you have forgotten this,
   everything which happens,
   always happened so
   and will happen so,
      and now happens so everywhere;

forgotten this too, how close is the kinship between
   one person and the whole human race,
      for it is a community, not of a little blood or seed,
      but of intelligence.

And you have forgotten this too,
    that everyone's intelligence is a god, and
    is an efflux of the deity;

and forgotten this, that nothing is one's own,
    but that his child and his body and his very soul
    came from the deity;

forgotten this, that everything is opinion;

and lastly you have forgotten
    that everyone lives the present time only,
        and loses only this.

MARCUS AURELIUS

Look upon physical and mental suffering as gifts.
  They bring their own lesson such as the
  temporalness of life,
  and the intrinsic worth of the eternal;.

Do not become disheartened and alarmed
  when adversity, calamity and misfortune
  fall upon you, for those who have acquired the
  power of enduring adversities,
  can enter the spiritual path.

Do not fear suffering or blame others.
  According to the law that governs the Universe,
  all sufferings are your labour of love
  to unveil your real self.

In comparison to realising infinite bliss,
  all the suffering and agonies you experience
    amount to practically nothing.

MEHER BABA

Difficulties are precisely what makes
change and ascent possible.

Without them we should all have gone
to permanent sleep long ago.

RODNEY COLLIN
The Theory of Conscious Harmony

The Seventh Elegy
(excerpt)

Nowhere, Beloved, will world be but
    within us. Our life
passes in transformation. And the
    external
shrinks into less and less. Where once
    an enduring house was,
now a cerebral structure crosses our
    path, completely
belonging to the realm of concepts, as
    though it still stood in the brain.
Our age has built itself vast reservoirs
    of power,
formless as the straining energy that it
    wrests from the earth.

Temples are no longer known. It is we
    who secretly save up
these extravagances of the heart.
    Where one of them still survives,
a Thing that was formerly prayed to,
    worshipped, knelt before -
just as it is, it passes into the invisible
    world.
Many no longer perceive it, yet miss
    the chance
to build it inside themselves now, with
    pillars and statues: greater.

RAINER MARIA RILKE
The Seventh Elegy (excerpt)
Translated by Stephen Mitchell

There is nothing without
that was not at the same time within us.

If the divine spark were not native to us,
how could it move us to rapture?

J.W. VON GOETHE

t Anne, the Virgin and the Infant Christ (detail)
LEONARDO DA VINCI, Louvre, Paris

Imagine someone living in the depths of the sea.
He might think that he was living on the surface, and
seeing the sun and the other heavenly bodies through
the water, he might think that the sea was the sky.
He might be so sluggish and feeble that he had never
reached the top of the sea, never emerged and raised
his head from the sea into this world of ours,
and seen for himself - or even heard from someone who
had seen it - how much purer and more beautiful
it really is than the one in which his people live.

Now we are in just the same position.

PLATO

Ah yes
we are alone;
it is no use hiding it from ourselves.

PETRARCH

Every man has a religion:
    has something in heaven or earth which he will give
    up everything else for - something which absorbs him,
    possesses itself of him, makes him over into its image:
    something:

it may be something regarded by others as
    being very paltry, inadequate, useless:
    yet it is his dream, it is his lodestar,
    it is his master,

That, whatever it is,
    seized upon me, made me its servant, slave:
    induced me to set aside the other ambitions:
    a trail of glory in the heavens,
    which I followed, followed, with a full heart.
    When once I am convinced I never let go:

I had to pay much for what I got
   but what I got made what I paid for it
   much as it was
   seem cheap.

I had to give up health for it
   — my body — the vitality of my physical self:
   oh! much had to go
   — much that was inestimable, that no man should
   give up until there is no longer any help for it

..and what did I get for it?

I never weighed
   what I gave for what I got
   but I am satisfied with what I got.

WALT WHITMAN

Sometimes, by letting go we allow
some grace to enter by another channel,
which all our mental efforts
have hitherto kept out.

RODNEY COLLIN
The Theory of Conscious Harmony

The more still, more patient and more open we are when
    we are sad, so much the deeper and so much the
    more unswervingly does the new go into us,
    so much the better do we make
    it ours, so much the more will be *our* destiny,

and when on some later day it 'happens'
    (that is, steps forth out of us to others),
    we shall feel in our innermost selves
    akin and near to it.

    And that is necessary.

It is necessary -
    and toward this our development
    will move gradually -
    that nothing strange should befall us,
    but only that which has long belonged to us.

RAINER MARIA RILKE
Letters To A Young Poet
Translated by M.D. Herter Norton

Remember that you behave as at a banquet.
Is anything brought round to you?
Put out your hand and take a moderate share.
Doth it pass you by? Do not stop it.
Is it not yet come? Do not yearn in desire
towards it, but wait until it reaches you.

Be so with regard to children, wife, office, and
riches, and you will sometime be worthy to feast
with the Gods.

And if you do not so much as take the things
which are set before you, but are able even to
forego them, you will not only be worthy to feast
with Gods
        but to rule with them.

EPICTETUS

Give me beauty within the inward soul;
and may the outward and the
inward man be at one.
May I reckon the wise to be wealthy, and
may I have such a quantity of gold as
none but the temperate can carry.

That prayer, I think, is enough for me.

SOCRATES

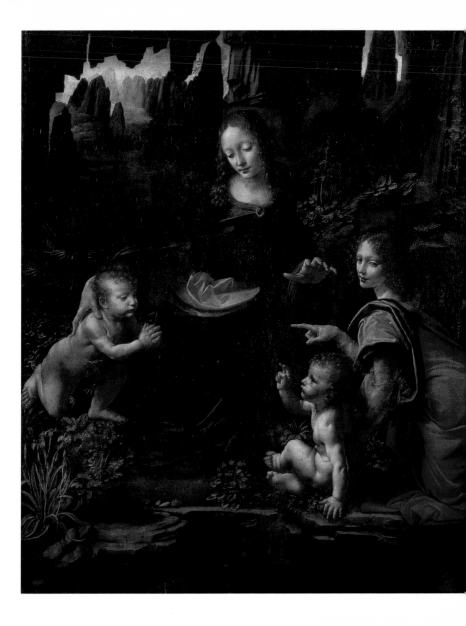

That which is excellent endures.

ARISTOTLE

The Virgin of the Rocks
LEONARDO DA VINCI, Louvre, Paris

When all is said and done,
one knows what one knows
only for oneself.

J.W. VON GOETHE

Great is the quality of truth in man,
The quality of truth in man supports itself through all changes,
It is inevitably in the man....He and it are in love, and never
leave each other.

The truth in man is no dictum....it is vital as eyesight,
If there be any soul there is truth....if there be man or woman
there is truth....If there be physical or moral there is truth,

If there be equilibrium or volition there is truth....if there be
things at all upon the earth there is truth.

O truth of the earth! O truth of things! I am determined to press
the whole way toward you,
Sound your voice! I scale mountains or dive in the sea after you.

WALT WHITMAN

O Light Eternal fixed in Self alone,
known only to Yourself, and knowing Self,
You love and glow, knowing and being known!

That circling which, as I conceived it, shone
in You as Your own first reflected light
when I had looked deep into It a while,

seemed in Itself and in Its own Self-color
to be depicted with man's very image.
My eyes were totally absorbed in It.

As the geometer who tries so hard
to square the circle, but cannot discover,
think as he may, the principle involved,
so did I strive with this new mystery:
I yearned to, know how could our image fit
into that circle, how could it conform;
but my own wings could not take me so high -
then a great flash of understanding struck my mind,
and suddenly its wish was granted.

At this point power failed high fantasy
but, like a wheel in perfect balance turning,
I felt my will and my desire impelled

by the Love that moves the sun and the other stars.

DANTE ALIGHIERI

If we do nothing in this life,
   the next life will be just the same,
   or there will be slight variations
   but no positive change.

There is only one thing we can change;
   we can try to awaken
   and hope to remain awake.
   If we have to come back, we cannot stop it.

We are in a train, the train is going somewhere.
   All we can do is to pass the time in the train
   differently - do something useful
      or spend it quite uselessly.

P.D. OUSPENSKY
Last words of the Fourth Way.

If people always remember that they cannot
lose by experiment,
they can only lose by trying nothing,
much can be learned.

RODNEY COLLIN
The Theory of Conscious Harmony

The blend of joy and sorrow that confounds us,
　　Sends us to earth: to veil our troubled state,
　　For benefice of Spring we supplicate.

And so I turn, the sun upon my shoulders,
　　To watch the water-fall, with heart elate,
　　The cataract pouring, crashing from the boulders,
　　Split and rejoined a thousand times in spate;
　　The thundrous water seethes in fleecy spume,
　　Lifted on high in many a flying plume,
　　Above the spray-drenched air. And then how splendid
　　To see the rainbow rising from this rage,
　　Now clear, now dimmed, in cool sweet vapour blended.
　　So strives the figures on our mortal stage.

This ponder well, the mystery closer seeing;
　　In mirrored hues we have our life and being.

J.W. VON GOETHE

Cartoon for St. Anne, the Virgin, the Infant Christ and the Young St. John (detail)
LEONARDO DA VINCI, The National Gallery, London

But, please consider whether these
great sadnesses have not rather gone
right through the centre of yourself?
Whether much in you has not altered,
whether you have not somewhere,
at some point of your being,
undergone a change while you were sad?

Were it possible for us to see further than
our knowledge reaches,
perhaps we would endure our sadnesses
with greater confidence than our joys.
For they are the moments when something
new has entered into us, something unknown;
our feelings grow mute in shy perplexity,
everything in us withdraws, a stillness comes,
and the new, which only one knows,
stands in the midst of it
        and is silent.

RAINER MARIA RILKE
from Letters To A Young Poet
Translated by M.D. Herter Norton

Profile of a Young Woman
LEONARDO DA VINCI, Galleria Degli Uffizi, Florence

To a good man, whether he lives or dies,
no event can be evil;
seeing that his concerns are never
disregarded by the gods.

Nor does what now happens to me
happen without a purpose on their part,
for I am persuaded that it is best for me to die
and to have done with the things of this world.

And I feel no anger either towards those who
have condemned me or towards my accusers.

LAST WORDS OF SOCRATES BEFORE
HIS EXECUTION BY POISONING.

Fate is fixed irrevocably by the Gods.

AESCHYLUS

The present moment is the point of escape
   from our three-dimensional prison of
   space and time.

For in this *present moment*,
   remembering oneself,
   one can put oneself in contact
   with a place outside time,
   and with the help of eternity,
   where all possibilities in their fullness
   are already waiting.

We must squeeze all its contents out of each moment.

RODNEY COLLIN
The Theory of Conscious Harmony

Trust no future, however pleasant!
Let the dead Past bury its dead!
Act -
Act in the living Present.
Heart within,
and God O'erhead!

HENRY WADSWORTH LONGFELLOW

When you realise and become firmly
   convinced that things could not be different,
   you cease to argue.

Arguing is based on the idea that things could
   be different and that some people could do things
   differently.

Try to think from the point of view that
   all that happens happens
   because it cannot be different;
   if it could be different it would have happened
   differently.

   It is very simple, but very difficult to realise.

P.D. OUSPENSKY

No human matter is of serious importance.

PLATO

Take therefore no thought for the morrow;
for the morrow shall take thought for
things of itself.

Sufficient unto the day
is the evil thereof.

MATTHEW 6:34

Finish every day and be done with it.
   You have done what you could. Some
   blunders and absurdities no doubt crept in;
   forget them as soon as you can.

Tomorrow is a new day; begin it well
   and serenely and with too high a spirit to
   be cumbered with your old nonsense.

This day is all that is good and fair.
   It is too dear, with its hopes and invitations,
   to waste a moment on the yesterdays.

RALPH WALDO EMERSON

How dear you are to me,
  you nights of sorrow.
    Why do I not kneel more to receive you,
      and give myself more loosely unto you.

    We, wasters of sorrow.
      How we gaze beyond them into some
        drab duration
          to see if they may not end there.

RAINER MARIA RILKE

Portrait of an Old Woman (detail)
REMBRANDT HARMENSZ VAN RIJN, Pushkin Museum, Moscow

If a man could understand all the horror of the lives
of ordinary people who are turning round in a
circle of insignificant interests and insignificant aims,
if he could understand what they are losing,
he would understand that there can only
be one thing that is serious for him -
to escape from the general law, to be free.

What can be serious for a man in prison who is
condemned to death?

Only one thing: how to save himself,
how to escape:
nothing else is serious.

G.I. GURDJIEFF

O thou that sleepest, what is sleep?
Sleep resembles death.
Ah, why then dost thou not work in such wise
that after death thou mayest retain a
resemblance to perfect life,
rather than during life make thyself
like the hapless dead
    by sleeping?

LEONARDO DA VINCI

All the world's a stage,
    And all the men and women merely players:
    They have their exits and their entrances;
    And one man in his time plays many parts,
    His acts being seven ages. At first the infant,
    Mewling and puking in the nurse's arms.
    And then the whining school-boy, with his satchel,
    And shining morning face, creeping like snail
    Unwilling to school. And then the lover,
    Sighing like furnace, with a woeful ballad
    Made to his mistress' eyebrow. Then a soldier,
    Full of strange oaths, and bearded like the pard,
    Jealous in honour, sudden and quick in quarrel,
    Seeking the bubble reputation
    Even in the cannon's mouth.

And then the justice,
In fair round belly with good capon lined,
With eyes severe, and beard of formal cut,
Full of wise saws and modern instances;
And so he plays his part. The sixth age shifts
Into the lean and slipper'd pantaloon,
With spectacles on nose and pouch on side,
His youthful hose well saved, a world too wide
For his shrunk shank; and his big manly voice,
Turning again toward childish treble, pipes
And whistles in his sound. Last scene of all,
That ends this strange eventful history,
Is second childishness and mere oblivion,
Sans teeth, sans eyes, sans taste, sans every thing.

WILLIAM SHAKESPEARE
As You Like It

My Lord, may I so rule others with my sceptre
that I govern myself by thy word;
in guiding the state, may the soul so
dominate the flesh,
reason dominate the soul,
faith dominate reason,
thy grace dominate faith,
that nothing may please me
which is displeasing to thee,
nothing be wise to me
which is not in accord with thy word.

PRAYER OF QUEEN ELIZABETH I

Two rules we should always have ready:

There is nothing good or evil
save in the Will;

and

We are not to lead events,
but to follow them.

EPICTETUS

Remember that you are an actor
in a drama of such sort as the author
chooses,

If short, then in a short one;
if long, then in a long one.

If it be his pleasure that you should enact
a poor man,
see that you act it well; or a cripple,
or a ruler, or a private citizen.

For this is your business,
to act well a given part;
but to select it belongs to another.

EPICTETUS

Most of our actions are low comedy.
   We must enact our part duly, but as the
   part of a borrowed character.

Of the mask and appearances we must not
   make a real essence,
      nor of what is foreign what is our very own.
   We cannot distinguish the skin from the shirt.

It is enough to decorate our face,
   without decorating our heart.

MICHEL MONTAIGNE

$\mathbf{W}$e are made free,
not by refusing to recognise any thing above us,
but on the contrary
by *revering* something that is above us.

For by revering it we rise to its level,
and by our recognition we attest the fact
that we ourselves bear within us
the stamp of the higher existence
and are capable of achieving it.

J.W. VON GOETHE

t. John the Baptist (detail)
ΕΟΝΑRDO DA VINCI, Louvre, Paris

$\mathcal{A}$ thousand times I have ascertained
and found it to be true
that the universe and the
affairs of the universe
are totally
  nothing into nothing.

HAFIZ

Our revels now are ended. These our actors,
As I foretold you, were all spirits, and
Are melted into air, into thin air:
And, like the baseless fabric of this vision,
The cloud-capp'd towers, the gorgeous palaces,
The solemn temples, the great globe itself,
Yea, all which it inherit, shall dissolve,
And like the insubstantial pageant faded,
Leave not a rack behind.

We are such stuff as dreams are made on,
and our little life is rounded with a sleep.

SHAKESPEARE
The Tempest

$\mathfrak{M}$an must sacrifice his suffering.

"What could be easier to sacrifice?" everyone will say.
But in reality people would sacrifice anything rather
than their negative emotions. There is no pleasure and
no enjoyment man would not sacrifice for quite small
reasons, but he will never sacrifice his suffering.
And in a sense there is a reason for this.

In a quite superstitious way man expects to gain
something by sacrificing his pleasures, but he cannot
expect anything for sacrifice of his suffering.
He is full of wrong ideas about suffering - he still
thinks that suffering is sent to him by God or
by Gods for his punishment or for his edification,
and he will even be afraid to hear of the possibility of
getting rid of his suffering in such a simple way.

P.D. OUSPENSKY
The Psychology of Man's Possible Evolution

If our misfortunes be great,
the strength of mind with which we have
to bear up against them must be likewise great.

The life of man is a continuous struggle and
a field of work where he rarely finds rest.

He has hardly entered upon it when the battle begins.

PETRARCA

$\mathcal{B}$egin to search and dig in thine own field
for this pearl of eternity that lies in it.
It cannot cost thee too much
nor canst thou buy it too dear,
for it is all.

And when thou hast found it,
thou wilt know that
all thou has sold or given away for it
is a mere nothing
as a bubble upon the water.

WILLIAM LAW

Will you never perceive what you are,
    or for what you were born,
        or for what purpose you are admitted
            to behold this spectacle?

EPICTETUS

Forget the day that has been cut off
from thy existence;
disturb not thyself about tomorrow,
which has not yet come:
rest not upon that which is no more;
live happily one instant
and throw not thy life to the winds.

OMAR KHAYYAM

Accept what the present brings and live in that.

If one is not established in the present
then one is nowhere and
nothing is possible.

RODNEY COLLIN
The Theory of Conscious Harmony

Remind yourself that what you love is mortal,
that you love what is not your own.
It is allowed for the present,
not irrevocably, not forever,
but is as a fig or a cluster of grapes
in the appointed season.

EPICTETUS

The Jewish Bride (detail)
REMBRANDT HARMENSZ VAN RIJN, Rijksmuseum, Amsterdam

Follow through!

The only attitude by which everything is
accomplished;
why is it so rarely sustained?

Why is it so difficult to create in ourselves and
those we try to influence?

J.W. VON GOETHE

$\mathcal{D}$esire is when you do what you want;

$\mathcal{W}$ill is when you can do what you do not want.

P.D. OUSPENSKY

Various are the fates sent by the Gods,
and much comes to us that is unexpected;

   on the one hand,
what we looked for is not accomplished;

   and on the other,
they find a way to bring about
              what we least expected.

EURIPIDES

There is no such thing as chance,
and what seems to us the merest accident
springs from the deepest
source of destiny.

FRIEDRICH SCHILLER

How small a part of the boundless
and unfathomable time is assigned to every man?
For it is very soon engulfed in the eternal.

And how small a part of the whole substance?
And upon what a small clod of
the whole Earth thou creepest?

Reflecting on all this, consider nothing to be great.

MARCUS AURELIUS

Not marble, nor the gilded monuments
Of princes, shall outlive this powerful rhyme;
But you shall shine more bright in these contents
Than unswept stone, besmear'd with sluttish time.
When wasteful war shall statues overturn,
And broils root out the work of masonry,
Nor Mars his sword nor war's quick fire shall burn
The living record of your memory.
'Gainst death and all-oblivious enmity
Shall you pace forth; your praise shall still find room
Even in the eyes of all posterity
That wear this world out to the ending doom.
So, till the judgement that yourself arise,
You live in this, and dwell in lovers' eyes.

WILLIAM SHAKESPEARE
Sonnets LV

You can understand other people only as much
as you understand yourself
and *only on the level of your own being.*

This means that you can judge other people's
knowledge but you cannot judge their being.
You can see in them only as much as you have
in yourself. But people always make the mistake
of thinking that they can judge other people's being.

In reality, if they wish to meet and *understand*
people of higher development than themselves
they must work with the aim of changing their
being.

P.D. OUSPENSKY
The Psychology of Man's Possible Evolution

You cannot understand and disagree.

P.D. OUSPENSKY

$\mathbf{W}$hat is the way out?

I believe, to put oneself completely
in the hands of higher powers,
    to be happy to be silent.

RODNEY COLLIN

La Donna Scapigliata
LEONARDO DA VINCI, GALLERIA NAZIONALE, Parma

If only we arrange our life according to
    that principle which counsels us that
        we must always hold to the difficult,
    then that which now still seems to us
    the most alien
    will become what we must trust and
    find most faithful.

How should we be able to forget those
    ancient myths about dragons that
    at the last moment turn into princesses;
    perhaps all the dragons of our lives are
    princesses who are only waiting to
    see us once beautiful and brave.

Perhaps everything terrible is
    in its deepest being something helpless
    that wants help from us.

RAINER MARIA RILKE
*from Letters To A Young Poet
Translated by M.D. Herter Norton*

$\mathbf{I}$t is existing, but not living,
to keep ourselves bound and obliged
by necessity to a single course.

The fairest souls are those that have
the most variety and adaptability.

MICHEL MONTAIGNE

I wish to persuade you, if I can,
to change your mind,

that, instead of a life of intemperate craving
which can never be satisfied,
choose a temperate life which is
content with whatever comes to hand
    and asks no more.

SOCRATES

Wishing relates to the end,
choice to the means;
for instance, we wish to be healthy,
but do we choose the acts which will make us healthy,
and we wish to be happy and say we do,

but we cannot well say we choose to be so;
for in general, choice seems to relate to the things
that are in our own power.

ARISTOTLE

We have to admit that unhappiness, painful experiences, and even obvious mistakes can teach us much.

Taken in the right way these same failures and discomforts can be the raw material of which understanding and will are made.

The reconstruction of one's life does not of necessity mean that such difficulties must be avoided.

On the contrary, it might imply that we face the difficulties that in this life we tend to avoid.

RODNEY COLLIN
The Theory of Conscious Harmony

Evolution depends on man's attitude:
if he accepts suffering and tries not to
    identify with it.

It may be that this whole law
was created so that he could become
stronger,

because strength can only be created by suffering.

P.D. OUSPENSKY
The Fourth Way

The spirit,
alive and gifted,
focusing with practical intent on
the most immediate concerns,
is the finest thing up on the earth.

J.W. VON GOETHE

Self-Portrait c.1661-62
REMBRANDT HARMENSZ VAN RIJN.
The Iveagh Bequest, Kenwood House, London

Look, contemplate the pearl of sorrow,
for it contains the wings of Psyche,
which carry us away from here.

HANS CHRISTIAN ANDERSEN

Girl Leaning on a Windowsill (detail)
REMBRANDT HARMENSZ VAN RIJN, Dulwich Picture Gallery, London

Love and be bold;
for he that dies hath these for wings
to rise from earth to heaven.

MICHELANGELO BUONARROTI

From
The Sonnets to Orpheus

Be ahead of all parting, as though it already were
behind you, like the winter that has just gone by.
For among these winters there is one so endlessly winter
that only by wintering through it will your heart survive.

Be forever dead in Euridice - more gladly arise
into the seamless life proclaimed in your song.
Here, in the realm of decline, among momentary days
be the crystal cup that shattered even as it rang.

Be - and yet know the great void where all things begin,
the infinite source of our inmost vibration,
so that , this once, you may give it your perfect assent.

To all that is used-up, and to all the muffled and dumb
creatures in the world's fools reserve, the unsayable sums,
joyfully add yourself, and cancel the count.

RAINER MARIA RILKE
Sonnet II,13
Translated by Stephen Mitchell

The Rubaiyat of Omar Khayyam
(excerpts)

I

Awake! for Morning in the Bowl of Night
Has flung the Stone that puts the Stars to Flight:
    And Lo! the Hunter of the East has caught
The Sultan's Turret in a Noose of Light.

II

Dreaming when Dawn's Left Hand was in the Sky
I heard a Voice within the Tavern cry,
    "Awake, my Little ones, and fill the Cup
Before Life's Liquor in its Cup be dry."

III

And, as the Cock crew, those who stood before
The Tavern shouted - "Open then the Door!
    You know how little while we have to stay,
And, once departed, may return no more."

VII

Come, fill the Cup, and in the Fire of Spring
The Winter Garment of Repentance fling:
The Bird of Time has but a little way
To fly - and Lo! the Bird is on the Wing.

XII

"How sweet is mortal Sovranty!" think some;
Others - "How blest the Paradise to come!"
Ah, take the Cash in hand and waive the Rest;
Oh, the brave Music of a distant Drum!

XXIV

Alike for those for TO-DAY prepare,
And those that after a TO-Morrow stare,
A Muezzin from the Tower of Darkness cries
"Fools! your Reward is neither Here nor There!"

XXVI

Oh, come with old Khayyam, and leave the Wise
To talk; one thing is certain, that Life flies;
One thing is certain, and the Rest is Lies;
The Flower that once has blown for ever dies.

XXXII

There was a Door to which I found no Key:
There was a Veil past which I could not see:
Some little Talk awhile of ME and THEE
There seem'd - and then no more of THEE and ME.

XXXVII

Ah, fill the Cup:- what boots it to repeat
How Time is slipping underneath our Feet:
Unborn TO-MORROW, and dead YESTERDAY
Why fret about them if TO-DAY be sweet!

XLV

But leave the Wise to wrangle, and with me
The Quarrel of the Universe let be;
And, in some corner of the Hubbub coucht,
Make Game of that which makes as much of Thee.

XLVI

For in and out, above, about, below,
'Tis nothing but a Magic Shadow-show
Play'd in a Box whose Candle is the Sun,
Round which we Phantom Figures come and go.

XLVII

And if the Wine you drink, the Lip you press,
End in the Nothing all Things end in - Yes -
Then fancy while Thou art, Thou art but what
Thou shalt be - Nothing - Thou shalt not be less.

XLIX

'Tis all a Chequer-board of Nights and Days
Where Destiny with Men for Pieces plays:
Hither and thither moves, and mates, and slays,
And one by one back in the Closet lays.

L

The Ball no Question makes of Ayes and Noes,
But Right or Left as strikes the Player goes;
And He that toss'd Thee down into the Field,
He knows about it all - HE knows - HE knows!

LI

The Moving Finger writes; and, having writ,
Moves on: nor all thy Piety nor Wit
Shall lure it back to cancel half a Line,
Nor all thy Tears wash out a Word of it.

LII

And that inverted Bowl we call The Sky,
Whereunder crawling coop't we live and die
Lift not thy hands to It for help - for It
Rolls impotently on as Thou or I.

LX

And, strange to tell, among the Earthen Lot
Some could articulate, while others not:
And suddenly one more impatient cried -
"Who is the Potter, pray, and who the Pot?"

LXXIII

Ah, Love! could thou and I with Fate conspire
To grasp this sorry Scheme of Things entire,
Would not we shatter it to bits - and then
Re-mould it nearer to the Heart's Desire!

FROM THE RUBAIYAT OF OMAR KHAYYAM
Translated by Edward Fitzgerald

The physical body was given man at birth by
Nature.

Somewhere exists the original Divine spark
launched from God
and which, refound,
will be his conscious spirit.

RODNEY COLLIN
The Theory of Conscious Harmony

The Virgin of the Rocks (detail)
LEONARDO DA VINCI, The National Gallery, London

One must not try to cling to opportunities which have come, however pleasant and comforting.

For that is the way to kill them.

Let good things go without regret.
Then better ones may come.

RODNEY COLLIN
The Theory of Conscious Harmony

Vex not thy spirit at the course of things:
they heed not thy vexation.

How ludicrous and outlandish
is astonishment at anything that
may happen in life.

MARCUS AURELIUS

The kingdom of heaven is like unto a
merchant man, seeking goodly pearls:
who, when he had found one pearl of great price,
went and sold all that he had,
and bought it.

MATTHEW 13:45

One must find something in himself
that longs above everything to grow,
to struggle,
     to wake up.

RODNEY COLLIN
The Theory of Conscious Harmony

Everything 'happens'. People can 'do' nothing.
From the time we are born to the time we die
things happen, happen, happen,
and we think we are doing.

This is our normal state in life, and even the
smallest possibility to do something comes only
through the work, and first only in oneself,
not externally.

Even in oneself 'doing' very often begins
by *not* doing. Before you can do something that
you cannot do, you must *not* do many things
which you did before.

For instance you cannot awake by just wanting to
awake, but you can prevent yourself sleeping
too much and too long.

P.D. OUSPENSKY

O ME! O life! of the questions of these recurring,
Of the endless trains of the faithless, of cities fill'd
with the foolish,
Of myself forever reproaching myself,
(for who more foolish than I, and who more faithless?)
   Of eyes that vainly crave the light, of the objects mean,
of the struggle ever renew'd,
   Of the poor results of all, of the plodding and sordid
crowds I see around me,
   Of the empty and useless years of the rest, with the rest
me intertwined,
   The question, O me! so sad, recurring-
What good amid these, O me,
      O life?

Answer.
   That you are here-that life exists and identity,
   That the powerful play goes on,
         and you may contribute a verse.

WALT WHITMAN
O ME! O Life!

*A*ll that is important
comes in quietness
and waiting.

RODNEY COLLIN
The Theory of Conscious Harmony

From
The Sonnets to Orpheus

Silent friend of many distances, feel
how your breath is still increasing space.
Among the beams of the dark belfries
let yourself ring out. What feeds on you

will grow strong upon this nourishment.
Be conversant with transformation.
From what experience have you suffered most?
Is drinking bitter to you, turn to wine.

Be, in this immeasurable night,
magic power at your senses' crossroad,
be the meaning of their strange encounter.

And if the earthly has forgotten you,
say to the still earth: I flow.
To the rapid water speak: I am.

RAINER MARIA RILKE
Sonnet II,29

We ought, so far as it lies within our power,
    to aspire to immortality,
       and do all that we can to live in conformity
       with the highest that is within us;

      For even if it is small in quantity,
       in power and preciousness
        it far excels all the rest.

ARISTOTLE

The Baptism of Christ (detail)
LEONARDO DA VINCI, Galleria Degli Uffizi, Florence

We think that negative emotions are produced by
circumstances, whereas all negative emotions
are *in us, inside us.* This is a very important point.

We always think our negative emotions are
produced by the fault of other people or by the fault
of circumstances. We *always* think that. Our negative
emotions are in ourselves and are produced by ourselves.

There is absolutely not a single unavoidable reason
why somebody else's action or some circumstance
should produce a negative emotion *in me.* It is only
my weakness. No negative emotions can be produced
by external causes if we do not want it.

We have negative emotions because we permit them,
justify them, explain them by external causes, and
in this way we do not struggle with them.

P.D. OUSPENSKY
The Fourth Way

It is rare for one to find a life
  that is well-ordered privately.

Any man can play his part in the side shows
  and represent a worthy man on the boards;
  but to be disciplined within, in his own bosom,
  where all is permissible and where all is
  concealed, that is the point.

MICHEL MONTAIGNE

And I say to mankind, Be not curious about God,
   For I who am curious about each am not curious about God,
   (No array of terms can say how much I am at peace about
God and about death.)

I hear and behold God in every object, yet understand
   God not in the least,
   Nor do I understand who there can be more wonderful
than myself.

Why should I wish to see God better than this day?
   I see something of God each hour of the twenty-four,
      and each moment then,
   In the faces of men and women I see God, and in my
      own face in the glass,
   I find letters from God dropt in the street, and every one
      is sign'd by God's name,
   And I leave them where they are, for I know that
      wheresoe'er I go,
   Others will punctually come for ever and ever.

WALT WHITMAN
Excerpt from Song of Myself

Alas, two souls are living in my breast,
And one wants to separate itself from the other.
One holds fast to the world with earthy passion
And clings with twining tendrils:
The other lifts itself with forceful craving
To the very roof of heaven.

J.W. VON GOETHE
Faust

Man cannot move, think, or speak
of his own accord. He is a marionette
pulled here and there by invisible strings.
If he understands this, he can learn more about
himself, and possibly then things may begin
to change for him.

But if cannot realise and understand
his *utter mechanicalness*,
or if he does not wish to accept it as a fact,
he can learn nothing more, and things cannot
change for him.

MAN *is a machine*, but a very peculiar machine.
He is a machine which, in right circumstances
and with right treatment, *can know that he
is a machine*, and, having fully realised this,
he may find the ways
to cease to be a machine.

P.D. OUSPENSKY

Every man shift for all the rest
and let no man take care
for himself
for all is but fortune.

WILLIAM SHAKESPEARE

The philosophy of six thousand years has
    not searched the chambers and magazines
    of the soul.

In its experiments there has always
    remained, in the last analysis, a
    residuum it could not resolve:
    Man is a stream whose source is hidden.
    Always our being is descending into us
    from we know not whence.

I am constrained every moment to
    acknowledge a higher origin for events
    than the will I call mine.

RALPH WALDO EMERSON
The Over-Soul

W̲hosoever strives against heaven-sent calamities
is striving in folly.

What must be, cannot be changed.

Things as they are,
Myself as I am.

RODNEY COLLIN
The Theory of Conscious Harmony

Rembrandt Self-Portrait 1669
REMBRANDT HARMENSZ VAN RIJN, The National Gallery, London

Suffering interrogates life.

It ask questions about our daily way of life,
about its direction
   and its ultimate meaning.

KRISTIAAN DEPOORTERE

We must learn to suffer what we cannot evade.

Our life, like the harmony of the world, is composed
of contrary things
-of diverse tones, sweet and harsh, sharp and flat,
    sprightly and solemn:

The musician who should only like some of these, what
would he be able to do? He must know how to use them all
    and to blend them.

And so should we mingle the goods and evils which are
consubstantial with our life.
Our being cannot survive without this mixture,
    and the one part is no less necessary to it than the other.

MICHEL MONTAIGNE.

And so the mystery remains
that we have sorrow so we can understand joy;
failure so we can recognize success;
   pain, so we can relish pleasure.

Somehow, built into the mystery
of this duality in life
is a blueprint for growth that has the potential
for shaping us into the people
   who God wants us to be.

ANTOINETTE BOSCO

Someone passes through your life and leaves an image
that you cannot forget, nor find comfort from.

But did you not leave such a trace in some other person's life,
without caring or even knowing?
    Did I not, did not everyone?

Everything must work itself out. All debts must be paid.
All one has inflicted one has to suffer,
before one can become free.

So those who wish for freedom can only say.
    " Let what comes come: I will accept it. "

RODNEY COLLIN

This universe where we are living,
   and of which we form a tiny particle,
   is the distance put by Love between God and God.

   We are a point in this distance.
   Space, time, and the mechanism that
   governs matter are the distance.

   Everything that we call evil is only this mechanism.

SIMONE WEIL

We must accept our existence as far as ever it is possible;
everything, even the unheard of, must be possible there.

That is fundamentally the only courage
which is demanded of us:
to be brave in the face of the strangest,
most singular and most inexplicable things
that can befall us.

RAINER MARIA RILKE

Let us not weigh in the grudging scales the merits and
demerits of our fellow man,
but let us think only of their need-
of the sorrows, the difficulties, perhaps the blindnessess,
   that make the misery of their lives;

Let us remember that they are fellow- sufferers in the
same darkness,
   actors in the same tragedy with ourselves.

SIMONE WEIL

Do you not see how necessary a world of pains and
troubles is to school an Intelligence and make it a Soul?
A place where the heart must feel and suffer in a
thousand diverse ways!

Not merely is the heart a textbook, it is the mind's Bible,
it is the mind's experience, it is the teat from which
the mind or intelligence sucks its identity.

As various as the lives of men are, so various become
their souls and thus does God make individual beings,
Souls of the sparks of his own essence.

For what are circumstances but provings of man's heart,
which are fortifiers and alterers of his nature?

JOHN KEATS

But to avoid danger
is so often to avoid opportunity,
    and he who successfully hides from the devil
very often hides from God too.

RODNEY COLLIN
The Theory of Conscious Harmony

The necessary thing is after all but this:
solitude, great inner solitude.
Going-into-oneself and for hours meeting
no one - this one must be able to attain.
To be solitary, the way one was solitary as
a child, when the grown ups went around
involved with things that seemed important
and big because they themselves looked so busy
and because one comprehended nothing of their doings.

And when one day one perceives
that their occupations are paltry,
their professions petrified and no longer linked with
living, why not then continue to look like a child
upon it all as upon something unfamiliar,
from out of the depth of one's own world,
out of the expanse of one's own solitude,
which is itself work and status and vocation?

RAINER MARIA RILKE
from Letters To A Young Poet
Translated by M.D. Herter Norton

All man's well-being depends upon two things:
one is the right choice of aim,
   of the end to which actions should tend,

the other lies in the finding of the actions
   that lead to that end.

ARISTOTLE

He who promises lightly
   must be lacking in faith.

He who thinks everything is easy
   will end by finding everything difficult.

Therefore, the Sage, who regards everything
   as difficult,

   meets with no difficulties in the end.

LAO TZU
Tao Te Ching

Man must suffer whatever Destiny
and the relentless Fate spun for him
with the first thread of life
when he came from his mother's womb.

HOMER

So teach us to number our days,
That we may apply our hearts unto wisdom.

PSALMS 90:12

I have seen great beauty of spirit in some who
   were great sufferers.

I have seen men, for the most part, grow better
   not worse with advancing years,

and I have seen the last illness produce treasures of
fortitude and meekness from the most unpromising subjects....

If the world is indeed a "vale of soulmaking,"
it seems on the whole
   to be doing its work.

C. S. LEWIS

Suffering is perhaps the only wellspring of genuine love
in the human person.

Does not the mystery of evil and suffering consist in this,
that without suffering, people would no longer know
what love is
and would no longer be capable of it!

To Love is essentially to suffer with another.
Where there is no suffering,
love, too, has been banished.

BERNARD KEMP

Time present and time past
Are both perhaps present in time future,
And time future contained in time past.
If all time is eternally present
All time is unredeemable.
What might have been is an abstraction
Remaining a perpetual possibility
Only in a world of speculation.
What might have been and what has been
Point to one end, which is always present.
Footfalls echo in the memory
Down the passage which we did not take
Towards the door we never opened
Into the rose-garden. My words echo
Thus, in your mind.
                    But to what purpose
Disturbing the dust on a bowl of rose-leaves
I do not know.
                    Other echos
Inhabit the garden. Shall we follow?
Quick, said the bird, find them, find them,
Round the corner. Through the first gate,
Into our first world, shall we follow
The deception of the thrush? Into our first world

There they were, dignified, invisible,
Moving without pressure, over the dead leaves,
In the autumn heat, through the vibrant air,
And the bird called, in response to
The unheard music hidden in the shrubbery,
And the unseen eyebeam crossed, for the roses
Had the look of flowers that are looked at.
There they were as our guests, accepted and accepting.
So we moved, and they, in a formal pattern,
Along the empty alley, into the box circle,
To look down into the drained pool.
Dry the pool, dry concrete, brown edged,
And the pool was filled with water out of sunlight,
And the lotus rose, quietly, quietly,
The surface glittered out of heart of light,
And they were behind us, reflected in the pool.
Then a cloud passed, and the pool was empty.
Go, said the bird, for the leaves were full of children,
Hidden excitedly, containing laughter.
Go, go, go, said the bird: Human kind
Cannot bear very much reality.
Time present and time future
What might have been and what has been
Point to one end, which is always present.

TS ELIOT
BURNT NORTON

Nowhere, my love, can there be a world
but within us.
Our life passes through changing
and ever fainter dwindles
the external.

RAINER MARIA RILKE

It has been well said that no man ever sank under
   the burden of the day.
It is when tomorrow's burden is added to the burden of today
   that the weight is more than a man can bear.

Never load your selves so.
If you find yourselves so loaded, at least remember this:
It is your own doing, not God's.

Leave the future to him and mind the present.

GEORGE MACDONALD

Life is about losing everything.

ISABEL ALLENDE

Have you learned lessons only of those who admired you,
and were tender with you, and stood aside for you?
Have you not learned great lessons from those
who braced themselves against you, and
   disputed the passage with you?

WALT WHITMAN
Leaves of Grass

In seeking know thyself,-
So shalt thou become they being.

But if thou cease from seeking,
Whatever thou hast, whatever thou art,
This will itself take away from thee:
True being of thy being.

RUDOLF STEINER

Show me, O Lord, my life's end and the number of my days;
let me know how fleeting is my life.
You have made my days a mere handbreadth;
the span of my years is as nothing before you.
Each man's life is but a breath.

Man is a mere phantom as he goes to and fro:
he bustles about, but only in vain;
he heaps up wealth, not knowing who will get it.

But now, Lord, what do I look for?
My hope is in You.

PSALM 39

Character cannot be developed in peace and quiet.

Only through the experience of trial and suffering
can the soul be strengthened, vision cleared,
ambition inspired,
and success achieved.

HELEN KELLER

We are coming to see that every success has
necessarily to be paid for by high percentage of failure.
There is no progress in being without some
mysterious tribute of tears, blood and sin.

It is not to be wondered at, then, if, as we look around us,
there are some shadows which grow deeper
as the light grows stronger:

for, when we look at it from this angle, suffering, in
all its forms and all its degrees, is
(at least partially) no more than the natural consequence
of the very movement by which we ourselves
are brought into being.

PIERRE TEILHARD DE CHARDIN

To live is to fight.

SENECA

$\mathbf{B}$e kind,

for everyone you meet is fighting a hard battle.

PHILO

Night is drawing nigh.
For all that has been - Thanks!
To all that shall be - Yes!

DAG HAMMARSKJOLD

One man succeeds in everything and so it loses all;
another meets with nothing but crosses and
disappointments and thereby gains
more than all the world is worth.

These few reflections sufficiently show us that the
different conditions of this life have
nothing in them to excite our uneasy passions,
nothing than can reasonably interrupt our love
and affection to one another.

WILLIAM LAW

Acknowledgements

~

I wish to express my deepest gratitude to Robert Burton, a spiritual teacher of the ancient system of the Fourth Way, for introducing me to a higher quality of life through the appreciation of fine impressions, art, music and beauty. I am grateful to him for his profound teachings which have stimulated and influenced my thoughts to aspire to my highest spiritual possiblities.

My warmest thanks to the many students of the Fellowship of Friends around the world who have contributed directly and indirectly to this book through selections in journals and other publications, and through their Being.

Especially, my grateful thanks to Stephen Swales, Mark Hutchinson-Braun and Malcolm Cohan for contributions of quotations.

To Liz Seymour and Glyn Jowsey my thanks for their unerring patience and help when circumstances prevented me from making the printing deadline.

To my parents, Pam and Roy Hayward and to Pat Cowan my deep thanks for their loving support, and for always being there to help.

To my husband, Malcolm, my deep appreciation for his help and guidance, suggestions, friction, for pushing me through the intervals, and for his belief in doing things for your Being.

And of course my love to my darling children, Zaky and Autumn, for giving me many hours of solitude to work on this book and for their loving encouragement at a time when producing Being took precedence over all else.

~

Art Resources
& Permissions

Grateful acknowledgement is made to RANDOM HOUSE INC. for permission to reprint excerpts from *The Selected Poetry of Rainier Maria Rilke*, translated by Stephen Mitchell (Viking 1989), and for excerpts of *The Theory of Conscious Harmony* by Rodney Collin (1987), and to W.W. Norton & Company for permission to reprint excerpts from *Sonnets to Orpheus* by Rainier Maria Rilke, translated by M.D. Herter Norton (1934, 1954).

Grateful acknowledgement is made to the following:

Bridgeman Art Gallery, London, for reproductions of LEONARDO DA VINCI: *The Baptism of Christ; The Annunciation; Self-Portrait 1661-62; Girl Leaning on a Windowsill, Portrait of an Old Woman; Self-Portrait 1657;* RAPHAEL: *The School of Athens;* and FRA ANGELICO: *Detail of Angel Beating a Drum*

Agence Photographique de la Reunion des Musees Nationaux, Paris, for permission and reproductions of LEONARDO DA VINCI: *The Virgin, The Infant Jesus and St Anne; The Virgin, the Infant Christ and the Young St. John;* and *St. John the Baptist;*

The Rijksmuseum, Amsterdam for permission and reproductions of REMBRANDT: *The Jewish Bride;* and *Titus in friar's habit 1661;*

Trustees of the The National Gallery, London, for permission and reproductions of REMBRANDT: *Self-Portrait (Age 63);* LEONARDO DA VINCI: *The Virgin of the Rocks;* and *Cartoon for St. Anne, the Virgin, the Infant Christ and the Young St. John;*

The Trustees of the The Royal Collection at the Windsor Castle for permission and reproduction of LEONARDO DA VINCI: *Head of a Woman;*

Scala Art Resource, Florence, for permission and reproductions of LEONARDO DA VINCI: *Profile of a Young Woman;*

GALLERIA NAZIONALE, Parma, for permission and reproductions of LEONARDO DA VINCI: *La Donna Scapigliata.*

Every effort has been made by the publishers to source and identify copyright on the selections herein. The publishers apologise for any instance where copyright has been inadvertently ommitted or incorrectly acknowledged. Any errors which will be rectified in future reprints.

Bibliography
& Suggested Reading

ARISTOTLE
Introduction to Aristotle (Modern Library Series) by Richard McKeon 1992.
The Complete Works of Aristotle: The Revised Oxford Translation (Bollingen Series)
    by Jonathan Barnes (Editor). Published by Princeton University Press 1984.

AESCHYLUS
Aeschylus. Published by Cambridge University Press 1992..

RODNEY COLLIN
The Theory of Celestial Influence — Man, the Universe, and Cosmic Mystery.
    London 1954, Stuart & Watkins.
The Theory of Conscious Harmony—From the Letters of Rodney Collin.
    London 1958, Vincent Stuart.

DANTE ALIGHIERI
Meditations with Dante Alighieri by James Collins. Bear & Company 1984.
Paradiso by Dante Alighieri (Modern Library Series) 1996.

FRA ANGELICO
Fra Angelico (Library of the Great Masters) Published by Riverside Book Co 1990.

ROBERT EARL BURTON
Self-Remembering. Published by Samuel Weiser 1995.

RALPH WALDO EMERSON
Essays and Poems. Everyman's Library 1995

EPICTETUS
The discourses: a classical guide to freedom and happiness.
    Published by B. & L. Cooper 1986.
Enchiridion (Great Books in Philosophy) Published by Prometheus Books 1955

JOHANN WOLFGANG VON GOETHE
Italian Journey {1786-1788} (Penguin Classics) by J.W. Goethe, W.H. Auden, E. Mayer.

Johann Wolfgang von Goethe. Published by Penguin USA 1992.

Johann Wolfgang Von Goethe Selected Poems.
  Published by John Calder Pub Ltd 1988

Conversations with Goethe by Johann Wolfgang von Goethe
  Published by Dent; Dutton.

G.I. GURDJIEFF
All and Everything in three series:
  First Series: Beelzebub's Tales to His Grandson. Routledge & Kegan Paul, 1991.
  Second Series: Meetings with Remarkable Men. Viking Penguin, 1991.
  Third Series: Life is Real Only Then, When 'I Am'. Routledge & Kegan Paul. 1981

HAFIZ
FIFTY POEMS BY HAFIZ (edited by A.J. Arberry). Cambridge Univ Pr 1970.

HOMER
Homer: Iliad Xxiv. by C. W. MacLeod. Published by Cambridge University Press 1982.
Homer the Odyssey. Published by Cambridge University Press 1988.

LAO TZU
Tao Te Ching (Everyman's Library) 1994.

LEONARDO DA VINCI
Leonardo The Artist and The Man by Serge Bramly. Penguin 1992.
Leonardo da Vinci. An Artabras Book. Published by Reynal & Company in association
  with William Morrow 1985.

MARCUS AURELIUS
The Meditations of Marcus Aurelius (Shambhala Pocket Classics) George Long 1993.

MEHER BABA
Sparks of the Truth: From the Dissertations of Meher Baba
  NR Edition Published by Sheriar Pr 1972.

MICHELANGELO
Michelangelo and His World: Sculpture of the Italian Renaissance by Joachim Poeschke,
   Albert Hirmer (Photographer), Irmgard Ernstmeier-Hirmer. Published by Harry N Abrams 1996.

MILTON
The Complete Poetry of John Milton. Published by Doubleday 1971.

MONTAIGNE
Complete Essays of Montaigne by M.E. De Montaigne. Published by Stanford Univ Pr 1958.

OMAR KHAYYAM
The Rubaiyat of Omar Khayyam Explained by Paramhansa Yogananda. Crystal Clarity 1994.

P.D. OUSPENSKY
THE FOURTH WAY - A Record of Talks and Answers to Questions based on the Teaching of
   G. I. Gurdjieff. Routledge & Kegan Paul, 1981.
Conscience, The Search for Truth. London, Arkana 1988.
The Cosmology of Man's Possible Evolution. Agora Books 1989.
The Psychology of Man's Possible Evolution. New York, Knopf 1945.
A Further Record—Extracts from Meetings 1928-1945. Arkana 1945.
In Search of the Miraculous—Fragments of an Unknown Teaching.
   New York 1949, Harcourt; London 1950, Routledge & Kegan Paul.

PLATO
Complete Works by Plato, John M. Cooper (Editor), D. S. Hutchinson
   (Editor). Published by Hackett Pub Co 1997.

REMBRANDT
Rembrandt: Self Portrait by Pascal Bonafoux.
   Editions d' Art Albert Skira 1985.
Rembrandt by Annemarie Vels Heijn.
   Rijksmuseum and Scala Books 1989

Rembrandt by Jessica Hodge - Bison Books and Magna Books 1994.

Rainer Maria Rilke
Ahead of All Parting: The Selected Poetry and Prose of
    Rainer Maria Rilke. Stephen Mitchell (Editor/Translator) Modern Library 1995.
Duino Elegies. W W Norton & Co 1992.
The Selected Poetry of Rainer Maria Rilke, Stephen Mitchell (Editor) Vintage Books 1989.
Letters to a Young Poet. Translation by M.D. Herter Norton
    Published by W.W. Norton & Company, Inc. 1954

Socrates
Conversations of Socrates (Penguin Classics) by Xenophon, Hugh Tredennick,
    Robin Waterfield (Translator). Published by Penguin USA 1990.

The Buddha
Dhammapada by G Buddha, Irving Babbitt. Published by W W Norton & Co 1965.

The Holy Bible

Walt Whitman
Leaves of Grass. Published by Signet Classics (Penguin) 1980.

William Blake
Blake: Poems (Everyman's Library Pocket Poets) Published by Knopf 1994.

William Shakespeare
The Complete Works of William Shakespeare. Published by Outlet 1992.

William Wordsworth
Selected Poems (Everyman's Library) Damian Walford Davies (Editor) 1996.

About the Author

Susan Hayward is the creator of the best-selling trilogy A GUIDE
FOR THE ADVANCED SOUL, BEGIN IT NOW, and BAG OF
JEWELS. Her background is in Natural Therapies, Art and
Philosophy. She began her own publishing company, IN-TUNE
BOOKS, in 1984 as a way to combine her interest in philosophy
with her love of fine book-making, and to inspire other
souls on their paths to development.

BEING is the result of Susan's life-long exploration into the
esoteric meaning within great Art, Music and Literature, and its
influence on humanity.

Born in New Zealand, she now lives in Palm Beach, Australia
with her husband Malcolm and her three children.